W9-CJK-084

To

From

Words to Warm a Sister's Heart
© 2008 Summerside Press
www.summersidepress.com

Cover & Interior Design by
Müllerhaus Publishing Group | www.mullerhaus.net

All rights reserved. No part of this book may be reproduced in any form
without permission in writing from the publisher.

Scripture references are from the following sources: The Holy Bible,
New International Version® NIV®. © 1973, 1978, 1984 by International
Bible Society. Used by permission of Zondervan. The New King James
Version (NKJV). Copyright © 1982 by Thomas Nelson, Inc. Used by
permission. The Holy Bible, New Living Translation® (NLT). Copyright
© 1996, 2004. Used by permission of Tyndale House Publishers, Inc.,
Wheaton, Illinois. The Message © 1993, 1994, 1995, 1996, 2000, 2001,
2002 by Eugene Peterson. Used by permission of NavPress, Colorado
Springs, CO. The New Century Version® (NCV). Copyright © 1987,
1988, 1991 by Thomas Nelson, Inc. Used by permission. All rights
reserved.

Excluding Scripture verses, references to men and masculine pronouns
have been replaced with gender-neutral references.

ISBN 978-1-934770-41-2

Printed in China

WORDS TO WARM
· · · A · · ·
Sister's
HEART

summerside
PRESS

TABLE OF CONTENTS

You are God's Created Beauty

Let there be many windows in your soul,
That all the glory of the universe may beautify it.

ELLA WHEELER WILCOX

Stretch out your hand and take the world's wide gift of Joy and Beauty.

CORINNE ROOSEVELT ROBINSON

Today a new sun rises for me; everything lives,
everything is animated, everything seems to speak to me
of my passion, everything invites me to cherish it.

ANNE DE LENCLOS

The beauty of a woman is not in a facial mole,
But true beauty in a woman is reflected in her soul.
It is the caring that she lovingly gives,
the passion that she shows,
And the beauty of a woman
with passing years—only grows!

AUDREY HEPBURN

Something deep in all of us yearns for God's beauty,
and we can find it no matter where we are.

SUE MONK KIDD

Go outside, to the fields, enjoy nature and the sunshine,
go out and try to recapture happiness in yourself
and in God. Think of all the beauty that's still left in
and around you and be happy!

ANNE FRANK

Isn't it a wonderful morning?
The world looks like something God had just
imagined for His own pleasure.

LUCY MAUD MONTGOMERY

When God is personally present...we are transfigured...,
our lives gradually becoming brighter and more beautiful
as God enters our lives and we become like Him.

2 CORINTHIANS 3:17-18 THE MESSAGE

The beauty of the world about us is only according to
what we ourselves bring to it.

BERTHA LINDSAY

Nothing can compare to the beauty and greatness
of the soul in which our King dwells in His full majesty.
No earthly fire can compare with the light
of its blazing love. No bastions can compare
with its ability to endure forever.

TERESA OF AVILA

In all ranks of life the human heart yearns for the
beautiful, and the beautiful things that God makes
are His gift to all alike.

HARRIET BEECHER STOWE

You should clothe yourselves...with the beauty that
comes from within, the unfading beauty of a gentle and
quiet spirit, which is so precious to God.

1 PETER 3:4 NLT

A sister is one who knows you as you really are,
understands where you've been, accepts who you've
become, and still gently invites you to grow
into a beauty all your own.

*You are God's created beauty and the
focus of His affection and delight.*

JANET WEAVER SMITH

As God's workmanship, we deserve to be treated,
and to treat ourselves, with affection and affirmation,
regardless of our appearance or performance.

MARY ANN MAYO

The future belongs to those who believe
in the beauty of their dreams.

ELEANOR ROOSEVELT

Beauty puts a face on God.
When we gaze at nature,
at a loved one, at a work of art,
our soul immediately recognizes
and is drawn to the face of God.

Margaret Brownley

The Lord is all I need.
He takes care of me.
My share in life has been pleasant;
my part has been beautiful.

Psalm 16:5-6 ncv

May God give you eyes to see beauty
only the heart can understand.

The Joys We Share

How sweet the sound of sisters laughing together,
of sharing the joy of knowing each other so well.

If one is joyful, it means that one is faithfully living
for God, and that nothing else counts; and if one
gives joy to others, one is doing God's work.
With joy without and joy within, all is well.

JANET ERSKINE STUART

*Sisters are for sharing laughter
and wiping tears.*

The God of the universe—the One who created
everything and holds it all in His hands—created each
of us in His image, to bear His likeness, His imprint.
It is only when Christ dwells within our hearts,
radiating the pure light of His love through our
humanity that we discover who we are and what we
were intended to be. There is no other joy that reaches
as deep or as wide or as high—there is no other joy
that is more complete.

But let all who take refuge in You be glad; let them ever
sing for joy. Spread Your protection over them,
that those who love Your name may rejoice in You.

PSALM 5:11 NIV

Our hearts were made for joy.
Our hearts were made to enjoy the One
who created them. Too deeply planted to be
much affected by the ups and downs of life,
this joy is a knowing and a being known
by our Creator. He sets our hearts alight
with radiant joy.

The gift of friendship—both given and received—is joy,
love and nurturing for the heart. The realization that you
have met a soul mate…a kindred spirit…a sister…
a true friend…is one of life's sweetest gifts!

As we grow in our capacities to see and enjoy the joys
that God has placed in our lives, life becomes
a glorious experience of discovering His endless wonders.

Add to your joy by counting your blessings.

You will show me the path of life; in Your presence
is fullness of joy; at Your right hand
are pleasures forevermore.

PSALM 16:11 NKJV

If you don't understand how a woman could both love
her sister dearly and want to wring her neck at the same
time, then you were probably an only child.

LINDA SUNSHINE

The Lord has filled my heart with joy; I feel very strong
in the Lord.... I am glad because You have helped me!

1 Samuel 2:1 ncv

To be able to find joy
in another's joy,
that is the secret
of happiness.

Reach out and care for someone who needs the touch
of hospitality. The time you spend caring today will be a
love gift that will blossom into the fresh joy
of God's Spirit in the future.

Emilie Barnes

When hands reach out in friendship,
hearts are touched with joy.

How necessary it is to cultivate
a spirit of joy. It is a psychological truth
that the physical acts of reverence
and devotion make one feel devout.
The courteous gesture increases one's
respect for others. To act lovingly
is to begin to feel loving,
and certainly to act joyfully
brings joy to others which in turn
makes one feel joyful.
I believe we are called
to the duty of delight.

DOROTHY DAY

Blessings
Overflow

Sisters are blossoms
in the garden of life.

I wish I had a box,
the biggest I could find,
I'd fill it right up to the brim
with everything that's kind.
A box without a lock, of course,
and never any key;
for everything inside that box
would then be offered free.
Grateful words for joys received
I'd freely give away.
Oh, let us open wide a box
of praise for every day.

May the Lord, the God of your fathers, increase you
a thousand times and bless you as He has promised!

DEUTERONOMY 1:11 NIV

Let God's promises shine on your problems.

CORRIE TEN BOOM

*How great is God's goodness to have
given me a sister like you!*

Tarry at the promise till God meets you there.
He always returns by way of His promises.

L. B. COWMAN

Once someone held my hand
and wiped away a tear.
That someone very special was you,
my sister dear.

God has not promised sun without rain,
joy without sorrow, peace without pain.
But God has promised strength for the day,
rest for the labor, light for the way,
grace for the trials, help from above,
unfailing sympathy, undying love.

ANNIE JOHNSON FLINT

You go before me and follow me.
You place Your hand of blessing on my head.
Such knowledge is too wonderful for me,
too great for me to understand!

PSALM 139:5-6 NLT

*Within each of us,
just waiting to blossom,
is the wonderful promise
of all we can be.*

I will let God's peace infuse every part of today. As the
chaos swirls and life's demands pull at me on all sides,
I will breathe in God's peace that surpasses
all understanding. He has promised that He would set
within me a peace too deeply planted to be affected by
unexpected or exhausting demands.

A sister is one of the nicest things that
can happen to anyone.
She is someone to laugh with and share with,
to work with and join in the fun.
She is someone who helps in the rough times
and knows when you need a warm smile.
She is someone who will quietly listen
when you just want to talk for awhile.

How great is You   odness, which You have stored up
for those who fear   which You bestow in the sight of
men on thos   take refuge in You.

PSA   19 NIV

I thank God, my sister, for the bles   you are...for the
joy of your laughter...the comfort of   r prayers...
the warmth of your smile.

Lift up your eyes. Your heavenly Father waits to
bless you—in inconceivable ways to make your life
what you never dreamed it could be.

ANNE ORTLUND

Sometimes I must drive her crazy.
But she loves me anyway and never lets on.
She continues to guard my heart and nurture my soul.
My sister is a true blessing in my life.

BETTY PEARL HOOPER

A close relationship with a sister is more than
camaraderie or companionship; it's a familiarity
of our self, a touching of souls.

Someone to Laugh With

It was nice growing up with someone like you—someone
to lean on, someone to count on...someone to tell on!

I know my older sister loves me because
she gives me all her old clothes and
has to go out and buy new ones.

He will once again fill your mouth with laughter
and your lips with shouts of joy.

JOB 8:21 NLT

Sense of humor; God's great gift
causes spirits to uplift,
Helps to make our bodies mend;
lightens burdens; cheers a friend;
Tickles children; elders grin
at this warmth that glows within;
Surely in the great hereafter
heaven must be full of laughter!

If you can remain calm, you just don't have all the facts.

Take time to laugh.
It is the music of the soul.

A cheerful heart is good medicine.

PROVERBS 17:22 NIV

A sister is one who laughs at your jokes
when they're not very funny and
sympathizes with your problems
when they're not very serious.

You can kid the world. But not your sister.

CHARLOTTE GRAY

Whole-hearted, ready laughter heals, encourages,
relaxes anyone within hearing distance. The laughter that
springs from love makes wide the space around—gives
room for the loved one to enter in.

Eugenia Price

If I can be of any help,
you're in more trouble than I thought.

A good laugh is as good as a prayer sometimes.

Lucy Maud Montgomery

There's nothing wrong with having nothing to say,
as long as you don't say it out loud.

The best laughter, the laughter that can heal,
the laughter that has the truest ring, is the laughter that
flowers out of a love for life and its Giver.

Maxine Hancock

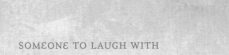

In the world you will have tribulation; but be of
good cheer, I have overcome the world.

JOHN 16:33 NKJV

To err is human, to blame your sister
even more so.

People can be divided into three groups:
those who make things happen,
those who watch things happen,
and those who wonder what happened.

If you can learn to laugh in spite of
the circumstances that surround you,
you will enrich others, enrich yourself,
and more than that, you will last!

BARBARA JOHNSON

If your sister is in a tearing hurry
to go out and cannot catch your eye,
she's wearing your best sweater.

PAM BROWN

Blessed are they who can laugh at themselves, for they
shall never cease to be amused.

Today's Forecast: Partly rational with brief
periods of coherent thought giving way
to complete apathy by tonight.

SHERRIE WEAVER

Ah ....
Contentment

The moments I love best
are the times I spend with you.

Contentment is not the fulfillment of what you want,
but the realization of how much you already have.

Where the soul is full of peace and joy,
outward surroundings and circumstances are
of comparatively little account.

HANNAH WHITALL SMITH

*Peace within
makes beauty without.*

ENGLISH PROVERB

We brought nothing into the world,
so we can take nothing out.
But, if we have food and clothes,
we will be satisfied with that.

1 TIMOTHY 6:7-8 NCV

• •

Normal day, let me be aware of the
treasure you are. Let me learn from you,
love you, bless you before you depart.
Let me not pass you by in quest
of some rare and perfect tomorrow.

The great advantage of living in a large family is that early
lesson of life's essential unfairness.

NANCY MITFORD

Life is not intended to be
simply a round of work,
no matter how interesting
and important that work may be.
A moment's pause to watch
the glory of a sunrise or a sunset
is soul satisfying, while a bird's song
will set the steps to music all day long.

LAURA INGALLS WILDER

Sometimes our hearts get tangled
And our souls a little off-kilter
Friends and family can set us right
And help guide us back to the light.

SERA CHRISTANN

Keep your lives free from the love of money and be
content with what you have, because God has said,
"Never will I leave you; never will I forsake you."

HEBREWS 13:5 NIV

I am still determined to be cheerful and happy,
in whatever situation I may be; for I have
also learned from experience that the greater part
of our happiness or misery depends upon our
dispositions, and not upon our circumstances.

MARTHA WASHINGTON

*It is always wise to stop wishing for
things long enough to enjoy the fragrance
of those now flowering.*

PATRICE GIFFORD

Let the day suffice,
with all its joys and failings,
its little triumphs and defeats.
I'd happily, if sleepily,
welcome evening as a time of rest,
and let it slip away, losing nothing.

KATHLEEN NORRIS

When it's hard to look back,
and you're scared to look ahead,
you can look beside you
and your sister will be there.

Godliness with contentment is great gain.

1 Timothy 6:6 nkjv

The desire to be and have a sister
is a primitive and profound one
that may have everything
or nothing to do with the family
a woman is born to. It is a desire
to know and be known by someone
who shares blood and body,
history and dreams, common ground
and the unknown adventures
of the future, darkest secrets
and the glassiest beads of truth.

Elizabeth Fishel

Love
All Around

Love is reaching, touching and caring,
sharing sunshine and flowers,
so many happy hours
together.

There is no need to plead that the love of God shall fill our
hearts as though He were unwilling to fill us....
Love is pressing around us on all sides like air. Cease to
resist it and instantly love takes possession.

AMY CARMICHAEL

Heaven comes down to touch us
when we find ourselves safe
in the heart of another.

Open your hearts to the love God instills....
God loves you tenderly. What He gives you is not to be
kept under lock and key,
but to be shared.

MOTHER TERESA

No matter how far apart we are,
I'll always be thinking of you, my sister,
because you mean the world to me.

What we have once enjoyed we can never lose. All that
we love deeply becomes a part of us.

HELEN KELLER

Loving a sister is an unconditional,
narcissistic, and complicated devotion
that approximates a mother's love...
sisters are inescapably connected,
shaped by the same two parents,
the same trove of memory and experience.

MARY BRUNO

Only He who created
the wonders of the world
entwines hearts in an eternal way.

Life's lasting joy comes in erasing
the boundary line between
"mine" and "yours."

Love makes burdens lighter,
because you divide them.
It makes joys more intense,
because you share them.
It makes you stronger,
so that you can reach out
and become involved with life
in ways you dared not risk alone.

A sister is someone who knows all about you, and still
chooses not to go away.

To love a person is to learn the song that is in their heart,
and to sing it to them when they have forgotten.
For You bless the Godly, O Lord;
You surround them with Your shield of love.

PSALM 5:12 NLT

Love...bears all things, believes all things, hopes all things,
endures all things. Love never fails.

1 CORINTHIANS 13:4, 7-8 NKJV

Nothing can separate you from His love, absolutely
nothing.... God is enough for time, and God is enough
for eternity. God is enough!

HANNAH WHITALL SMITH

Love grows from our capacity to give
what is deepest within ourselves
and also receive what is the deepest
within another person.
The heart becomes an ocean
strong and deep,
launching all on its tide.

Love God, your God, walk in all His ways, do what
He's commanded, embrace Him, serve Him with
everything you are and have.

Joshua 22:1 the message

Encouragment
Means
So Much

There are times when encouragement means such a lot.
And a word is enough to convey it.

GRACE STRICKER DAWSON

By now we know and anticipate one another so easily,
so deeply, we unthinkingly finish each other's sentences,
and often speak in code. No one else knows what I mean
so exquisitely, painfully well; no one else knows
so exactly what to say, to fix me.

JOAN FRANK

*When mom and dad don't understand,
a sister always will.*

Some days, it is enough encouragement
just to watch the clouds break up and disappear,
leaving behind a blue patch of sky
and bright sunshine that is so warm upon my face.
It's a glimpse of divinity;
a kiss from heaven.

For there is no friend like a sister
In calm or stormy weather;
To cheer one on the tedious way,
To fetch one if one goes astray,
To lift one if one totters down,
To strengthen whilst one stands.

CHRISTINA ROSSETTI

A word of encouragement to those we meet, a cheerful
smile in the supermarket, a card or letter to a friend,
a readiness to witness when opportunity is given—
all are practical ways in which we may let
His light shine through us.

ELIZABETH B. JONES

I'm sure now I'll see God's goodness in the
exuberant earth. Stay with God! Take heart. Don't quit.

PSALM 27:13 THE MESSAGE

More and more I realize that everybody, regardless of
age, needs to be hugged and comforted in a brotherly or
sisterly way now and then. Preferably now.

JANE HOWARD

Calm me, O Lord, as You stilled the storm,
Still me, O Lord, keep me from harm.
Let all the tumult within me cease,
Enfold me, Lord, in Your peace.

CELTIC TRADITIONAL

Encouragement is being a good listener, being positive,
letting others know you accept them for who they are.
It is offering hope, caring about the feelings
of another, understanding.

GIGI GRAHAM TCHIVIDJIAN

The comfort of knowing that our bond will survive despite our differences and that our connection provides each of us with a more accurate picture of ourselves enhances our chances of finding inner peace and satisfaction as we age together.

JANE MERSKY LEDER

Sisters lift our spirits and stick with us when times are tough.

May our Lord Jesus Christ Himself and God our Father encourage you and strengthen you in every good thing you do and say. God loved us, and through His grace He gave us a good hope and encouragement that continues forever.

2 THESSALONIANS 2:16 NCV

Hope begins in the dark, the stubborn hope that if you just show up and try to do the right thing, the dawn will come. You wait and watch and work: You don't give up.

ANNE LAMOTT

They have been a wonderful encouragement to me, as they have been to you. You must show your appreciation to all who serve so well.

1 CORINTHIANS 16:18 NLT

I wanted you to see what real courage is…. It's when you know you're licked before you begin but you begin anyway and you see it through no matter what.

HARPER LEE

To help one another, is part of the religion of sisterhood.

LOUISA MAY ALCOTT

Praise: a Perpetual Rejoicing

Happiness is a quiet, perpetual
rejoicing in small events.

God specializes in things fresh and firsthand. His plans
for you this year may outshine those of the past....
He's preparing to fill your days with reasons
to give Him praise.

JONI EARECKSON TADA

Let us give all that lies within us...to pure praise, to pure
loving adoration, and to worship from a grateful heart—
a heart that is trained to look up.

AMY CARMICHAEL

Our prayers should be burning words coming forth from
the furnace of a heart filled with love. Devoutly, with
great sweetness, with natural simplicity, without any
affectation, offer your praise to God with
the whole of your heart and soul.

MOTHER TERESA

Sing praise to the Lord, you who belong to Him.
Praise His holy name.

PSALM 30:4 NCV

They that trust the Lord
find many things to praise Him for.
Praise follows trust.

LILY MAY GOULD

May your life become one of glad and unending praise
to the Lord as you journey through this world,
and in the world that is to come!

TERESA OF AVILA

If I were to make a solemn speech
in praise of you, in gratitude, in deep affection,
you would turn an alarming shade of crimson
and try to escape. So I won't.
Take it all as said.

MARION C. GARRETTY

The gift of praise is the best gift
you can give your sister,
any time of the year.

Let's praise His name! He is holy, He is almighty. He is
love. He brings hope, forgiveness, heart cleansing,
peace and power. He is our deliverer and coming King.
Praise His wonderful name!

LUCILLE M. LAW

Thanksgiving puts power in living, because it opens the generators of the heart to respond gratefully, to receive joyfully, and to react creatively.

Heavenly Father, thank You for my wonderful family. Even though we are not perfect, I praise You for this group of people that You have ordained as those who will be closest to me.... Amen.

KIM BOYCE

We are Your people, the sheep of Your flock. We will thank You always; forever and ever we will praise You.

PSALM 79:13 NCV

Morning has broken like the first morning,
Blackbird has spoken like the first bird....
Praise with elation, praise every morning,
God's re-creation of the new day!

ELEANOR FARJEON

If we learn how to give of ourselves,
to forgive others, and to live with thanksgiving,
we need not seek happiness.
It will seek us.

Our thanksgiving today should include
those things which we take for granted,
and we should continually praise our God,
who is true to His promise,
who has provided and retained
the necessities for our living.

BETTY FUHRMAN

Enter into His gates with thanksgiving,
and into His courts with praise.
Be thankful to Him and bless His name.

PSALM 100:4 NKJV

A Treasury of Faith

Faith expects from God
what is beyond all expectations.

Sisters that hold each other accountable usually have a
deep, abiding, and open relationship…. Being aware that
a sister cares enough to make us accountable
creates a stronger bond.

If it can be verified, we don't need faith…. Faith is for
that which lies on the other side of reason. Faith is what
makes life bearable, with all its tragedies and ambiguities
and sudden, startling joys.

MADELEINE L'ENGLE

For I am bound with fleshly bands,
Joy, beauty, lie beyond my scope;
I strain my heart, I stretch my hands,
And catch at hope.

CHRISTINA ROSSETTI

Be alert. Continue strong in the faith. Have courage, and be strong.

1 CORINTHIANS 16:13 NCV

I think miracles exist in part as gifts and in part as clues that there is something beyond the flat world we see.

PEGGY NOONAN

Just as a prism of glass miters light and casts a colored braid, a garden sings sweet incantations the human heart strains to hear. Hiding in every flower, in every leaf, in every twig and bough, are reflections of the God who once walked with us in Eden.

TONIA TRIEBWASSER

Faith is not an effort, a striving, a ceaseless seeking,
as so many earnest souls suppose, but rather a letting go,
an abandonment, an abiding rest in God that nothing,
not even the soul's shortcomings, can disturb.

The day is done, the sun has set,
Yet light still tints the sky;
My heart stands still
In reverence,
For God is passing by.

RUTH ALLA WAGER

Ever since I first heard of your strong faith in the
Lord Jesus and your love for God's people everywhere,
I have not stopped thanking God for you.
I pray for you constantly.

EPHESIANS 1:15-16 NLT

We must drink deeply from the very Source the deep calm
and peace of interior quietude and refreshment of God,
allowing the pure water of divine grace to flow
plentifully and unceasingly from the Source itself.

MOTHER TERESA

*I believe in the sun even if it
isn't shining. I believe in love even when
I am alone. I believe in God even
when He is silent.*

Now faith is the substance of things hoped for,
the evidence of things not seen.

HEBREWS 11:1 NCV

So wait before the Lord. Wait in the stillness. And in that
stillness, assurance will come to you. You will know
that you are heard;...you will hear quiet words
spoken to you yourself, perhaps to your grateful
surprise and refreshment.

AMY CARMICHAEL

Faith means being sure of what we hope for...now.
It means knowing something is real, this moment,
all around you, even when you don't see it.
Great faith isn't the ability to believe long and far
into the misty future. It's simply taking God
at His word and taking the next step.

JONI EARECKSON TADA

Within each of us there is an inner place
where the living God Himself longs to dwell,
our sacred center of belief.

Heartfelt Prayers

Pour out your heart to God your Father.
He understands you better than you do.

I said a prayer for you today
And I know God must have heard,
I felt the answer in my heart
Although He spoke no word.
I asked that He'd be near you
At the start of each new day,
To grant you health and blessings
And friends to share the way.
I asked for happiness for you
In all things great and small,
But it was His loving care
I prayed for most of all.

Life is fragile—
handle with prayer.

When we call on God, He bends down His ear to listen,
as a father bends down to listen to his little child.

ELIZABETH CHARLES

I call on You, O God,
for You will answer me;
give ear to me and hear my prayer.
Show the wonder of Your great love,
You who save by Your right hand
those who take refuge in You.

PSALM 17:6-7 NLT

We must take our troubles to the Lord, but we must do
more than that; we must leave them there.

HANNAH WHITALL SMITH

Lord...give me the gift of faith to be renewed and
shared with others each day. Teach me to live this
moment only, looking neither to the past with regret,
nor the future with apprehension. Let love be my aim
and my life a prayer.

ROSEANN ALEXANDER-ISHAM

You pay God a compliment
by asking great things of Him

TERESA OF AVILA

You are helping us by praying for us. Then many
people will give thanks because God has
graciously answered so many prayers

2 CORINTHIANS 1:11 NLT

We need quiet time to examine our lives openly
and honestly...spending quiet time alone gives your mind
an opportunity to renew itself and create order.

SUSAN L. TAYLOR

If a care is too small to be turned into a prayer
then it is too small to be made into a burden.

It is when things go wrong, when good things
do not happen, when our prayers seem to have been lost,
that God is most present.

MADELEINE L'ENGLE

*Your life is the answer
to someone's prayers.*

As soon as I pray, You answer me;
You encourage me by giving me strength.

PSALM 138:3 NLT

God bless the friend who sees my needs
and reaches out a hand,
who lifts me up, who prays for me,
and helps me understand.

AMANDA BRADLEY

Open wide the windows of our spirits and fill us full
of light; open wide the door of our hearts that we may
receive and entertain Thee with all the
powers of our adoration.

CHRISTINA ROSSETTI

My sister is my strength
She hears the whispered prayers
That I cannot speak
She helps me find my smile,
Freely giving hers away
She catches my tears
In her gentle hands.

LISA LORDEN

Allow your dreams a place in your prayers and plans.
God-given dreams can help you move into the future
He is preparing for you.

BARBARA JOHNSON

Family
Connection

Within the property of our heart and soul
we find our sister; she is essential
to our memories, our connectedness, our being.

Call it clan, call it a network,
call it a tribe, call it a family.
Whatever you call it, whoever you are,
you need one.

JANE HOWARD

Families give us many things—
love and meaning, purpose and
an opportunity to give,
and a sense of humor.

It's hard to be responsible, adult, and sensible all the time.
How good it is to have a sister whose heart is
as young as your own.

PAM BROWN

We know one another's faults, virtues, catastrophes, mortifications, triumphs, rivalries, desires, and how long we can each hang by our hands to a bar. We have been banded together under pack codes and tribal laws.

ROSE MACAULAY

Family faces are magic mirrors. Looking at people who belong to us, we see the past, present, and future.

GAIL LUMET BUCKLEY

Having a sister is like having a best friend you can't get rid of. You know whatever you do, they'll still be there.

AMY LI

Please, bless my family. Let it continue before You always. Lord God, You have said so.

2 SAMUEL 7:29 NVC

We were a strange little band of characters,
trudging through life sharing diseases and toothpaste,
coveting one another's desserts, hiding shampoo,
borrowing money, locking each other out of our rooms,
inflicting pain and kissing to heal it in the same instant,
loving, laughing, defending, and trying to figure out the
common thread that bound us all together.

ERMA BOMBECK

Like branches on a tree we grow in different directions
yet our roots remain as one. Each of our lives will always
be a special part of the other.

Children of the same family, the same blood, with the
same first associations and habits, have some means of
enjoyment in their power, which no subsequent
connections can supply.

JANE AUSTEN

• • • • • • • • • • • • • • • • • • • •

You are citizens along with all of God's holy people.
You are members of God's family.

ΕPHESIANS 2:19 NLT

*We really need only five things on
this earth: Some food, some sun,
some work, some fun, and someone.*

BEATRICE NOLAN

The effect of having other interests beyond those
domestic works well. The more one does and sees and
feels, the more one is able to do, and the more genuine
may be one's appreciation of fundamental things like
home, and love, and understanding companionship.

AMELIA EARHART

Sooner or later we all discover that
the important moments in life
are not the advertised ones, not the birthdays,
the graduations, the weddings,
not the great goals achieved.
The real milestones are less prepossessing.
They come to the door of memory.

SUSAN B. ANTHONY

As for me and my family, we will serve the Lord.

JOSHUA 24:15 NCV

Sisters is probably the most competitive relationship
within the family, but once the sisters are grown,
it becomes the strongest relationship.

MARGARET MEAD

Our
Priorities

A sister listens to your deepest hurts
and feels they are hers too.

Choices can change our lives profoundly. The choice
to mend a broken relationship, to say yes to a
difficult assignment, to lay aside some important work to
play with a child, to visit some forgotten person—
these small choices may affect our lives eternally.

GLORIA GAITHER

*Getting things accomplished
isn't nearly as important
as taking time for love.*

JANETTE OKE

So be careful how you live. Don't live like fools, but like
those who are wise. Make the most of every opportunity
in these evil days. Don't act thoughtlessly, but understand
what the Lord wants you to do.

EPHESIANS 5:15-17 NLT

If I do one good thing today—for myself, for a sister
or brother, for the world—the day will be of value.

Be still, and in the quiet moments, listen to the voice
of your heavenly Father. His words can renew your
spirit...no one knows you and your needs like He does.

JANET WEAVER SMITH

Teach me, Father,
to value each day,
to live, to love,
to laugh, to play.

KATHI MILLS

The least of things with a meaning is worth more in life
than the greatest of things without it.

Make the most of every opportunity.
Be gracious in your speech.
The goal is to bring out the best in others.
COLOSSIANS 4:5 THE MESSAGE

Blessed is the person who is too busy to worry in the
daytime and too sleepy to worry at night.
CAROLINE SCHROEDER

Though two children have the same parents, the same
values, the same everything, they turn out different.
Isn't that the genius of God?

Live each day the fullest you can,
not guaranteeing there'll be a tomorrow,
not dwelling endlessly on yesterday.
JANE SEYMOUR

*A good example has twice
the value of good advice.*

If you look for Me wholeheartedly, you will find Me.

JEREMIAH 29:13 NLT

We must not, in trying to think about how we can make
a big difference, ignore the small daily differences we can
make which, over time, add up to big differences
that we often cannot foresee.

MARIAN WRIGHT EDELMAN

See each morning a world made anew, as if it were the
morning of the very first day;...treasure and use it, as if it
were the final hour of the very last day.

FAY HARTZELL ARNOLD

In some families, please is described as the magic word.
In our house, however, it was sorry.

Margaret Laurence

Time is a very precious gift of God;
so precious that it's only given to us
moment by moment.

Amelia Barr

Older sisters...listen to your secrets and anxieties.
And never tell—without your say-so.
An older sister is a friend and a defender—
a listener, conspirator, a counselor
and a sharer of delights....
A younger sister...is a valuable addition....
Someone who trusts you to defend her.
Someone who thinks you know the
answers to almost everything.

Pam Brown

Bonded in Friendship

Chance made us sisters, choice made us friends.
Our hearts have bonded in a friendship that is
full, rich, and soul-satisfying.

Friendship is the fruit gathered
from the trees planted in the
rich soil of love, and nurtured
with tender care and understanding.

ALMA L. WEIXELBAUM

Some friendships last a long, long time
while others quickly end,
But to have a loving sister
is to have a lifetime friend.

If we would build on a sure foundation in friendship,
we must love friends for their sake
rather than for our own.

CHARLOTTE BRONTË

Friends come and friends go,
but a true friend sticks by you like family.

PROVERBS 18:24 THE MESSAGE

Don't walk in front of me—I may not follow.
Don't walk behind me—I may not lead.
Walk beside me—And just be my friend.

We should all have one person
who knows how to bless us
despite the evidence.

PHYLLIS THEROUX

I am only as strong as the coffee I drink,
the hairspray I use,
and the friends I have.

Two are better than one, because they have
a good return for their work: If one falls down,
his friend can help him up.

ECCLESIASTES 4:9-10 NIV

Knowing what to say is not always necessary;
just the presence of a caring friend can make
a world of difference.

SHERI CURRY

A sister never asks you for a reason,
She never asks you why, or when?
A sister pays no heed to time or season,
She's a friend.
A sister never asks for only smiles and laughter,
She's there in gladness or in tears.
A sister's there, tomorrow and hereafter,
Through the years.

Insomuch as any one pushes you nearer to God,
he or she is your friend.

FRENCH PROVERB

Perhaps you'd be a bit surprised
how often, if you knew,
A joke, a song, a memory
will make me think of you.
It's like another moment
that we've really spent together,
Reminding me a sister is
a friend who's there forever.

*Our roots say we're sisters,
our hearts say we're friends.*

Perfume and incense bring joy to the heart,
and the pleasantness of one's friend
springs from his earnest counsel.

PROVERBS 27:9 NIV

A friend understands what you are trying to say...
even when your thoughts aren't fitting into words.

ANN D. PARRISH

A friend hears the song in my heart
and sings it to me when my memory fails.

Line by line, moment by moment, special times are
etched into our memories in the permanent ink
of everlasting relationships.

GLORIA GAITHER

Having someone who understands is a great blessing
for ourselves. Being someone who understands
is a great blessing to others.

JANETTE OKE

Provisions in Full Measure

Sisters are beyond price,
and there is no measuring of their goodness.

My sister's hands are fair and white;
my sister's hands are dark.
My sister's hands are touched with age,
or by the years unmarked.
And often when I pray for strength
to live as He commands
The Father sends me sustenance
in my sister's hands.

Sisters are angels who lend us
their wings when our wings have
forgotten how to fly.

If you have a special need today, focus your full attention
on the goodness and greatness of your Father rather
than on the size of your need. Your need is so small
compared to His ability to meet it.

One of the best things about being an adult is
the realization that you can share with your sister and still
have plenty for yourself.

BETSY COHEN

A father to the fatherless, a defender of widows,
is God in His holy dwelling.
God sets the lonely in families,
He leads forth the prisoners with singing....
You gave abundant showers, O God;
You refreshed Your weary inheritance.
Your people settled in it,
and from Your bounty, O God,
You provided for the poor.

PSALM 68:5-10 NIV

God's gifts make us truly wealthy. His loving supply
never shall leave us wanting.

BECKY LAIRD

You can trust God right now to supply all your needs
for today. And if your needs are more tomorrow,
His supply will be greater also.

*Provide me with
the insight that comes
only from Your Word.*

PSALM 119:169 THE MESSAGE

Throughout the Bible, when God asked a man to do
something, methods, means, materials and specific
directions were always provided.
The man had one thing to do: obey.

ELISABETH ELLIOT

You care for the land and water it;
You enrich it abundantly.
The streams of God are filled with water
to provide the people with grain,
for so You have ordained it.

PSALM 65:9 NIV

I must simply be thankful, and I am, for all the Lord has
provided for me, whether big or small
in the eyes of someone else.

MABEL P. ADAMSON

It is not my business to think about myself.
My business is to think about God.
It is for God to think about me.

SIMONE WEIL

You know full well as I do the value of
sisters' affections to each other;
there is nothing like it in this world.

CHARLOTTE BRONTË

There will be days which are great and everything goes
as planned. There will be other days when we aren't sure
why we got out of bed. Regardless of which kind of day it
is, we can be assured that God takes care
of our daily needs.

EMILIE BARNES

A sister by your side can keep you warmer
than the most expensive coat.

Celebrating Our Gifts

God gave me my gifts. I will do all I can
to show Him how grateful I am to Him.

GRACE LIVINGSTON HILL

A true friend inspires you to believe the best in yourself,
to keep pursuing your deepest dreams—most wonderful
of all, she celebrates all your successes
as if they were her own!

Since you are like no other being ever
created since the beginning of time,
you are incomparable.

BRENDA UELAND

God's designs regarding you, and His methods of bringing
about these designs, are infinitely wise.
MADAME JEANNE GUYON

Receiving a gift is like getting a rare gemstone;
any way you look at it, you see beauty refracted.
PROVERBS 17:8 THE MESSAGE

Each one of us is God's special work of art. Through us,
He teaches and inspires, delights and encourages,
informs and uplifts all those who view our lives.

JONI EARECKSON TADA

My sister is my future.
She lives within my dreams
She sees my undiscovered secrets,
Believes in me as I stumble
She walks in step beside me,
Her love lighting my way.

LISA LORDEN

Both within the family and without, our sisters hold up
our mirrors, our images of who we are and of who
we can dare to become.

ELIZABETH FISHEL

Give, and it will be given to you. A good measure,
pressed down, shaken together and running over, will be
poured into your lap. For with the measure you use,
it will be measured to you.

LUKE 6:38 NIV

God does not ask your ability or your inability.
He asks only your availability.

MARY KAY ASH

This is the real gift: you have been given the
breath of life, designed with a unique, one-of-a-kind
soul that exists forever—the way that you choose to
live it doesn't change the fact that you've been
given the gift of being now and forever.
Priceless in value, you are handcrafted by God,
who has a personal design and
plan for each of us.

Many persons have a wrong idea
of what constitutes true happiness.
It is not attained through self-gratification
but through fidelity to a worthy purpose.

HELEN KELLER

*Because He was full of grace and truth,
from Him we all received one gift
after another.*

JOHN 1:16 NCV

When I stand before God at the end of my life, I would
hope that I would not have a single bit of talent left and
could say, "I used everything You gave me."

ERMA BOMBECK

God has designs on our future...and He has
designed us for the future.
He has given us something to do in the future
that no one else can do.

RUTH SENTER

There are no limits to our opportunities.
Most of us see only a small portion of what is possible.
We create opportunities by seeing the possibilities
and having the persistence to act upon them.
We must always remember...opportunities are always
here, but we must look for them.

Sweet Simplicity

Sisters find the sweetest sense of happiness comes from simply being together.

Not every day of our lives is overflowing with
joy and celebration. But there are moments
when our hearts nearly burst within us
for the sheer joy of being alive.
The first sight of our newborn babies,
the warmth of love in another's eyes,
the fresh scent of rain on a hot summer's eve—
moments like these renew in us
a heartfelt appreciation for life.

GWEN ELLIS

Enjoy the little things.
One day you may look back and realize...
they were the big things.

A simple life in the Fear-of-God is better
than a rich life with a ton of headaches.

PROVERBS 15:16 THE MESSAGE

. . . .

It's simple things, like a glowing sunset, the sound
of a running stream or the fresh smell in a meadow that
cause us to pause and marvel at the wonder of life,
to contemplate its meaning and significance.
Who can hold an autumn leaf in their hand,
or sift the warm white sand on the beach,
and not wonder at the Creator of it all?

As different as my sister and I are, I need only to look in
the mirror and I see her eyes, her mouth, her expression;
then I remember all that we have in common.

LAURIE HARPER

Let us consider how we may spur one another on
toward love and good deeds. Let us not give up
meeting together, as some are in the habit of doing,
but let us encourage one another.

HEBREWS 10:24-25 NIV

My sister taught me everything
I really need to know, and she was only
in sixth grade at the time.

LINDA SUNSHINE

From the simple seeds
of understanding,
we reap the lovely harvest
of true friendship.

It isn't the great big pleasures that count the most;
it's making a great deal out of the little ones.

JEAN WEBSTER

Take time to notice all the
usually unnoticed, simple things in life.
Delight in the never-ending hope
that's available every day!

So in everything, do to others what you would have them
do to you, for this sums up the Law and the Prophets.

MATTHEW 7:12 NIV

A fiery sunset, tiny pansies by the wayside,
the sound of raindrops tapping on the roof—
what extraordinary delight we find
in the simple wonders of life!
With wide eyes and full hearts,
we may cherish what others often miss.

When you're growing up, a sister can be a readymade playmate...in old age, you've got someone who doesn't get bored by all your stories of the "good old days."

JANE DOWDESWELL

Happy people...enjoy the fundamental,
often very simple things of life....
They savor the moment, glad to be alive,
enjoying their work, their families,
the good things around them.
They are adaptable; they can bend with the wind,
adjust to the changes in their times, enjoy the
contest of life.... Their eyes are turned outward;
they are aware, compassionate.
They have the capacity to love.

JANE CANFIELD

God
Our Father

Because I have known you, my sister,
I know more of my God.

The God who created, names, and numbers the stars in
the heavens also numbers the hairs of my head.... He pays
attention to very big things and to very small ones.
What matters to me matters to Him,
and that changes my life.

ELISABETH ELLIOT

*The treasure our heart searches for
is found in the ocean of God's love.*

JANET WEAVER SMITH

Grace to you and peace from God our Father and
the Lord Jesus Christ.

ROMANS 1:7 NKJV

My Sister's Hands
My sister's hands: compassion's tools
that teach my own their art
Witnesses of charity
within the human heart
Bearers of the Savior's love
and mercy unto man
I have felt the Master's touch
in my sister's hands.

Whoever walks toward God one step,
God runs toward him two.

JEWISH PROVERB

Stand outside this evening. Look at the stars.
Know that you are special and loved by
the One who created them.

People who don't know God and the way He works
fuss over these things, but you know both God
and how He works. Steep yourself in God-reality,
God-initiative, God-provisions. You'll find all your
everyday human concerns will be met.
Don't be afraid of missing out. You're My
dearest friends! The Father wants to give you
the very kingdom itself.

LUKE 12:30-32 THE MESSAGE

The Creator thinks enough of you to have sent
Someone very special so that you might have life—
abundantly, joyfully, completely, and victoriously.

If nothing seems to go my way today,
this is my happiness:
God is my Father and I am His child.

BASILEA SCHLINK

Before anything else, above all else,
beyond everything else, God loves us.
God loves us extravagantly, ridiculously,
without limit or condition.
God is in love with us...God yearns for us.

ROBERTA BONDI

*God will never let you be shaken or
moved from your place near His heart.*

JONI EARECKSON TADA

When you love someone, you give to them, as God gives
to us. The greatest gift He ever gave was the person of
His Son, sent to us in human form so that we might know
what God the Father is really like!

DALE EVANS ROGERS

We continually recall before God our Father the things
you have done because of your faith and the work you
have done because of your love.

1 Thessalonians 1:3 ncv

God is every moment totally aware
of each one of us. Totally aware in intense
concentration and love.... No one passes through
any area of life, happy or tragic,
without the attention of God.

Eugenia Price

As a rose fills a room with its fragrance,
so will God's love fill our lives.

Margaret Brownley

The Simple Truth

There's a special kind of freedom sisters enjoy.
Freedom to share innermost thoughts,
to ask a favor, to show their true feelings.
The freedom to simply be themselves.

Wisdom is knowing the truth, and telling it.

Love is here and now, real and true,
the most important thing in our lives.
For love is the creator of our favorite memories
and the foundation of our fondest dreams.
Love is a promise that is always kept,
a fortune that can never be spent, a seed that
can flourish in even the most unlikely of places.
And this radiance that never fades,
this mysterious and magical joy,
is the greatest treasure of all—
one known only by those who love.

We may look old and wise to the outside world. But to
each other, we are still in junior [high] school.

CHARLOTTE GRAY

· ·

Amid ancient lore the Word of God stands unique
and pre-eminent. Wonderful in its construction,
admirable in its adaptation, it contains truths that a child
may comprehend, and mysteries into which
angels desire to look.

FRANCES ELLEN WATKINS HARPER

I am amazed by the sayings of Christ.
They seem truer than anything I have ever read.
And they certainly turn the world upside down.

KATHERINE BUTLER HATHAWAY

Then Jesus said..., "If you abide in My word, you are
My disciples indeed. And you shall know the truth,
and the truth shall make you free."

JOHN 8:31-32 NKJV

Open my eyes that I may see
Glimpses of truth Thou hast for me.
Place in my hands the wonderful key
That shall unclasp and set me free:
Silently now I wait for Thee,
Ready, my God, Thy will to see;
Open my eyes, illumine me, Spirit divine!

CLARA H. SCOTT

We shared. Parents. Home. Pets.
Celebrations. Catastrophes. Secrets.
And the threads of our experience
became so interwoven that we are linked.
I can never be utterly lonely,
knowing you share the planet.
I need news of you.
I need to know you're safe.
I need you.

PAM BROWN

Go after a life of love as if your life depended on it—
because it does. Give yourselves to the gifts God
gives you. Most of all, try to proclaim His truth.

1 CORINTHIANS 14:1 THE MESSAGE

*Truth is always exciting. Speak it, then.
Life is dull without it.*

PEARL S. BUCK

It is an extraordinary and beautiful thing
that God, in creation...works with
the beauty of matter; the reality of things;
the discoveries of the senses,
all five of them; so that we, in turn,
may hear the grass growing;
see a face springing to life
in love and laughter....
The offerings of creation...
our glimpses of truth.

MADELEINE L'ENGLE

Far away, there in the sunshine,
are my highest aspirations.
I may not reach them but I can look up
and see their beauty, believe in them,
and try to follow where they lead.

LOUISA MAY ALCOTT

Anyone who examines this evidence
will come to stake his life on this:
that God Himself is the truth.

JOHN 3:31 THE MESSAGE

My sister is my past.
She writes my history
In her eyes I recognize myself,
Memories only we can share.
She remembers, she forgives
She accepts me as I am
With tender understanding.

LISA LORDEN

A Grateful Spirit

Happiness is a healthy mental attitude,
a grateful spirit,
a clear heart full of love.

To receive a gift, molded from love and sacrifice,
selected with care and tied up with all the
excitement the giver has to offer, is indeed rare.
They don't come along often,
but when they do, cherish them.

ERMA BOMBECK

Seeing our Father in everything makes life one long
thanksgiving and gives a rest of heart, and, more than
that, a gayety of spirit, that is unspeakable.

HANNAH WHITALL SMITH

Thank You, Lord, for this chance to stretch some more in
Your direction—to trust You when I cannot understand.

QUIN SHERRER

Were there no God we would be in this glorious world
with grateful hearts and no one to thank.

CHRISTINA ROSSETTI

*That I am here
is a wonderful mystery
to which I will respond with joy.*

Let the peace of Christ rule in your hearts, since as
members of one body you were called to peace.
And be thankful. Let the word of Christ dwell in you
richly as you teach and admonish one another with all
wisdom, and as you sing psalms, hymns and spiritual
songs with gratitude in your hearts to God.

COLOSSIANS 3:15-16 NIV

A wonderful sister, a special friend,
that's what you've been to me...
so much a part of lovely times
I keep in memory.

Feeling grateful or appreciative of someone or something
in your life actually attracts more of the things that you
appreciate and value into your life. And, the more of your
life that you like and appreciate, the healthier you'll be.

CHRISTIANE NORTHRUP

Most of the people I know who have what I want—
which is to say, purpose, heart, balance, gratitude, joy—
are people with a deep sense of spirituality.... They are
part of something beautiful.

ANNE LAMOTT

*Thank you for the treasure
of your friendship…for showing me
God's special heart of love.*

Gratitude unlocks the fullness of life. It turns what we
have into enough, and more…. It can turn a meal into
a feast, a house into a home, a stranger into a friend.
Gratitude makes sense of our past, brings peace for today,
and creates a vision for tomorrow.

MELODY BEATTIE

Give thanks to the Lord, for He is good!
His faithful love endures forever.

1 CHRONICLES 16:34 NLT

Gratitude is the memory of the heart;
therefore forget not to say often,
I have all I ever enjoyed.

LYDIA MARIA CHILD

Lord, I thank You for answering me. You have saved me.

PSALM 118:21 NCV

Sisterhood is many things. It's a warm smile
on a cold and rainy day, a friendly hug,
a cheerful hello.... It's all that a good
and lasting friendship is, only better.
It's treasured. It's sacred. It's knowing that
there will always be someone there for you.
It's dreams shared, and goals achieved.
It's counting on others and being counted on.
It is real.

A Reflection of You

Walking through life with a sister gives you a special kind of counterpart—someone who reflects you so intrinsically but is still her own self.

• •

Trust in the Lord with all your heart,
and lean not on your own understanding;
in all your ways acknowledge Him,
and He shall direct your paths.

PROVERBS 3:5-6 NKJV

Sisters are our peers,
the voice of our times.

ELIZABETH FISHEL

The blossom cannot tell what becomes
of its fragrance as it drifts away,
just as no person can tell what becomes
of her influence as she continues through life.

120

Kindness is the only service that will stand the storm of life and not wash out. It will wear well and be remembered long after the prism of politeness or the complexion of courtesy has faded away.

The life-maps of God are right,
showing the way to joy.
The directions of God are plain
and easy on the eyes.

PSALM 19:7 THE MESSAGE

The fullness of our heart is expressed in our eyes,
in our touch, in what we write, in what we say,
in the way we walk, the way we receive,
the way we need.

MOTHER TERESA

Some people make the world special
just by being in it.

How blessed the man You train, God,
the woman You instruct in Your Word,
providing a circle of quiet within the clamor of evil....
God will never walk away from His people,
never desert His precious people.
Rest assured that justice is on its way
and every good heart put right.

PSALM 94:12-15 THE MESSAGE

A sister is a person
who has a sneaky knack
of saying good things about you
behind your back.

An older sister helps one remain
half child, half woman.

*The real secret of happiness
is not what you give
or what you receive,
it's what you share.*

Sisters—they share the agony and the exhilaration.
As youngsters they may share popsicles,
chewing gum, hair dryers, and bedrooms.
When they grow up, they share confidences,
careers and children, and some even chat
for hours every day.

ROXANNE BROWN

What we feel, think, and do this moment
influences both our present and the future
in ways we may never know.
Begin. Start right where you are.
Consider your possibilities and find inspiration...
to add more meaning and zest to your life.

ALEXANDRA STODDARD

A sister is dear to you always,
for she is someone who is always a part
of all the favorite memories
that you keep very close to your heart.

Unite
Our Hearts
in Wisdom

Nothing opens the heart like a sister with whom you may
share all your hopes, fears, and joys.

· · · · · · · · · · · · · · · · · · · ·

At the end of your life, you will never regret not having passed one more test, not winning one more verdict, or not closing one more deal. You will regret time not spent with a husband, a sister, a child, or a parent.

BARBARA BUSH

The wise don't expect to find life worth living; they make it that way.

True wisdom and power are found in God; counsel and understanding are His.

JOB 12:13 NLT

We ought to be able to learn things secondhand. There is not enough time for us to make all the mistakes ourselves.

HARRIET HALL

I am convinced beyond a shadow of any doubt that
the most valuable pursuit we can embark upon
is to know God.

KAY ARTHUR

My sister often knows the worst about me,
but she always believes in the best.

My sister's love is very special,
one I'll treasure through the years.
We've played and laughed together
and ofttimes shed many tears.
but through life's maze of problems,
God placed a bond of love within
To unite our hearts in wisdom
changing sisters into friends.

JUDY MEGGERS

Sisters touch your heart in ways no other could.
Sisters share...their hopes, their fears,
their love, everything they have.
Real friendship springs from their special bonds.

CARRIE BAGWELL

A wise gardener plants her seeds,
then has the good sense not to dig them up
every few days to see if a crop is on the way.
Likewise, we must be patient
as God brings the answers...
in His own good time.

QUIN SHERRER